Gospel Light's

SonTreasure Island VBS

Bible Story Center Guide

INCLUDES REPRODUCIBLE PAGES

MIDDLER ◇ AGES 8 TO 10 ◇ GRADES 3 AND 4

GOSPEL LIGHT VACATION BIBLE SCHOOL

Publishing Director, Donna Lucas
Associate Managing Editor, Karen McGraw
Editorial Team, Anne Borghetti, Mary Gross Davis
Production Manager, Peter Germann
Art Director, Lori Hamilton Redding
Senior Designer, Carolyn Thomas

Founder, Dr. Henrietta Mears
Publisher, William T. Greig
Senior Consulting Publisher, Dr. Elmer L. Towns
Editorial Director, Biblical and Theological Content, Dr. Gary S. Greig

Published by Gospel Light
Ventura, California, U.S.A.
All Rights Reserved. Printed in the U.S.A.

Contents

Teaching Helps

Sessions

Reproducible Pages

Evangelism Opportunity

This symbol highlights portions of the lessons that provide special opportunities to explain the gospel message to children. Look for this symbol in the Tell the Story section of each lesson.

SonTreasure Island
DISCOVERING GOD'S LOVE

COURSE DESCRIPTION

Who wouldn't want to explore a Caribbean island, with its glittering turquoise waters, warm white sands and cool ocean breezes? Visitors to SonTreasure Island are welcomed by the scent of exotic flowers, the taste of tropical fruits and the captivating sound of a steel-drum band. But this is no ordinary tropical escape! There is treasure to be found here. More precious than gold, more lasting than diamonds, it is the greatest treasure of all—God's love!

The Christian life begins with God's love for us and continues as His love flows through us to others. At SonTreasure Island, your treasure seekers will play island games, create colorful crafts and enjoy tropical snacks. But more importantly, they will discover the rich treasure of God's love through the truths found in 1 Corinthians 13.

Each day your children will learn how Jesus' life illustrates one of five key truths about God's love as described in this treasured passage of Scripture. They'll learn that because **God's Love Is Giving**, He sent His only Son, Jesus, to show His love to us. They will learn that Jesus helped a young girl and a sick woman because **God's Love Is Kind**. Through Jesus' compassion for a Samaritan woman, they will learn that **God's Love Is Caring**. Jesus' friendship with the tax collector Zacchaeus will show them that **God's Love Is Forgiving**. Finally, your children will discover that through Jesus' death and resurrection, we can know that **God's Love Is Forever**.

SUPPLY LIST

General Supplies
- Bible Story Posters for Sessions 1-5 from *Elementary Teaching Resources*
- SonTreasure Island CD and player
- SonTreasure Gem Stickers
- colored markers
- masking tape
- measuring stick
- Post-it Notes
- scissors

For each student—
- Bible
- *Treasure Guide*

Session 1
Coconut Connections
- Coconut Cards (p. 41)
- paper bag
- coconut (or other island object such as a toy fish, sturdy seashell, maraca, etc.)

Limber Limbo
- Limbo Cards (p. 42)
- broomstick

Tell the Story
- bag or box containing a personal treasure

Session 2
Swell Shells
- stopwatch or watch with second hand

For each pair of students—
- 6 seashells
- 2 paper plates

Pineapple Pick
- Pineapple Cards (p. 43)

For each team of 3 or 4 students—
- small paper plates in a variety of colors, including six yellow plates
- large bag

Session 3
Lifesaver Pass

For each student—
- toothpick
- 1 Lifesavers® candy (plus one extra for the class)

Fish Toss
- Fish Cards (p. 44)
- card stock
- large paper clips

For each team of 3 or 4 students—
- container (treasure chest, cardboard box, wastebasket, etc.)

Session 4
Building Sand Castles
- Sand Castle Patterns (pp. 45-46)
- card stock
- pencil
- sandpaper, brown construction paper or brown paper bags
- bucket
- large sheet of paper

Musical Map-Walk
- Map Puzzle (p. 47)
- stopwatch or watch with second hand

Session 5
Gem Hunt
- Gem Cards (p. 48)
- drinking straws

For each team of 3 or 4 students—
- a different color of paper
- container (treasure chest, cardboard box, wastebasket, etc.)

Beach Ball Volleyball
- yarn, clothesline or game net
- beach ball

Decorating Your Center

A few simple decorations can transform an ordinary classroom into part of SonTreasure Island. Use a variety of real items and/or painted backdrops. *Reproducible Resources* contains patterns and more detailed instructions. For additional information, see the decorating segment of the *Preview DVD*.

> For super quick and easy decorating, check out the posters in the Elementary Teaching Resources and the Decorating Poster Pack.

TREASURE POINT

Create a room full of treasure in your Bible Story Center. Use black electrical tape to make a large X on the floor. Add signs saying, "X marks the spot!" and "Ahoy! Ye found the buried treasure!" Paint signs on cardboard to look old and weathered, or use old pieces of wooden fencing. Suspend signs from the ceiling, or attach to entrance door.

As a focal point, set out a large treasure chest filled with jewels, coins and golden treasures. Use a real wooden trunk or chest, or construct a chest using cardboard boxes (see *Reproducible Resources*).

Arrange burlap fabric on the floor, placing boxes or crumpled newspaper underneath to make an uneven surface. Set the chest on a level spot on the burlap. (Optional: Scatter some sand on top of the burlap.) Fill the chest with crumpled paper. Then place treasure items on top.

For treasure, use plastic bead strings, acrylic jewels, discarded costume jewelry, play coins, and extra-large gold and silver sequins. Add ornate gold- and silver-colored items such as candlesticks, goblets and plates, or use metallic spray paint to paint items. Arrange objects to spill over the sides of chest and onto the burlap. Place several Bibles among the treasures. Prop an old rusted shovel against the wall.

Enlarge onto butcher paper the ship and dolphin patterns found in *Reproducible Resources*. Paint the patterns, cut out and attach to walls behind your treasure chest display. Cut out wavy pieces of blue butcher paper for the sea and attach to wall.

Create a huge treasure map of SonTreasure Island and place on one wall. Tape together two large sheets of white butcher paper. Paint the paper with brewed tea to give it an aged appearance. Draw a simple treasure map of SonTreasure Island. Then carefully singe (and quickly extinguish!) the edges of the map. Attach map to wall. Leave one wall free to hang Bible Story Posters during lessons.

Bible Story Center Basics

You play a very important part in VBS, whether you are the lead teacher in the Bible Story Center or a helper. The Bible Story Center is divided into three parts to help children learn important Bible truths.

Refer to the Bible Aims for each day as you prepare each lesson. The aims help you know what learning will be taking place during your lesson. Study the Teacher's Conclusion. This conversation provides an opportunity for evangelism.

This guide provides material for the Bible story. If you are also leading your class in other activities, refer to additional activity center guides (see back cover).

SET THE STORY (5-10 minutes)

If you only have 25 minutes for this center, you can omit Set the Story. Otherwise, choose either Option A or Option B as an introduction to the important Bible story concept. Or use them after the story for an active way to review the Bible concepts learned.

Option A

This brief group activity is designed for groups of 8 to 16 students. If you have more than 16 students, you can easily adapt the activity by duplicating it for an additional group of students—and adding another leader, of course!

Option B

This activity is similar in format to the Option A activity, but it has been written to provide an introduction to the session's Bible Memory Verse.

TELL THE STORY (10 minutes)

Each Bible story illustrates an aspect of God's love that Jesus taught by example. Display Bible story posters from *Elementary Teaching Resources* for children to see while listening to the story. Telling the story in small groups is ideal, but the story can be told effectively to a large group—just make sure additional staff members sit among children to guide children's behavior.

Introduction

Give Bibles to all students to use during the story. Consider beginning each story with a brief prayer. Then introduce the Bible story by asking a question that relates to familiar student experiences. This discussion helps children connect everyday life with the Bible lesson they are about to hear.

Bible Story

Each Bible story is written in language appropriate to the middler age level. (Note: If you are teaching a mixed age-level group, the version found in this *Middler Bible Story Center Guide* is most appropriate.) Each story also includes a Bible Storytelling Option to help you actively involve your listeners. During the story, volunteers read two or three Scripture passages from the Bible. This shows students exactly what God's Word says. See "Storytelling Tips" on page 10 for additional help.

For a fun alternative or supplement to the Bible story, ask teachers, helpers or student volunteers to perform the Bible story skits found in the *Assemblies & Skits Production Guide*.

Conclusion

After the main story, summarize the Bible truths for the children and relate the lesson to the aspect of God's love that students are learning about.

APPLY THE STORY (10-15 minutes)

Lead students in applying the lesson to their lives through discussion and activities in the *Treasure Guide*. This time includes

- Bible story review
- Memory verse discussion
- Application activity and discussion
- Silent and/or group prayer

Treasure Guides

Each session's *Treasure Guide* page contains a Bible story review activity and a memory verse activity. To reinforce the memory verse or reward students for verse memorization, SonTreasure Gem Stickers (available from Gospel Light) can be placed next to each memory verse.

Effective Teaching Tips

Preparation Is the Key

- Pray for God to prepare the hearts of your students.
- Be prepared before each day begins. Have all materials at hand, ready for use, so you can focus on the children and the learning that is taking place.
- Know the Lesson Focus for each day and use it to connect each activity to the lesson's Bible story and memory verse.
- Learn and practice good storytelling techniques. (See "Storytelling Tips" on page 10.)

Conversation Is an Art

- Be sensitive to each child's home situation and plan your conversation to include the variety of family situations represented in your class. Your conversations will help you discover what a child knows (or doesn't know) about a particular topic.
- Review the conversation suggestions provided. Think of ways you might tailor or build on these ideas to meet the needs of the students in your class. Write down any other ideas or questions you might ask, and keep them with you during the session.
- Plan to listen as much as you talk. Look directly at the child who is talking. Demonstrate your interest by responding to the specific ideas the child expressed.
- Know each child's name and use it in positive, loving, affirming ways throughout the lesson. Look for opportunities to express praise and encouragement.
- Be alert to ways of relating the present experience to what God's Word says, thus helping each child understand Bible truth.
- Stay with your students as they work. They need to know that you are there, ready to help and ready to listen.

Leading a Child to Christ

One of the greatest privileges of serving in VBS is helping children become members of God's family. Pray for the children you teach and ask God to prepare them to understand and receive the good news about Jesus. Ask God to give you the sensitivity and wisdom you need to communicate effectively and to be aware of opportunities that occur naturally.

Because children are easily influenced to follow the group, be cautious about asking for group decisions. Offer opportunities to talk and pray individually with any child who expresses interest in becoming a member of God's family—but without pressure. A good way to guard against coercing a child to respond is to simply ask, "Would you like to hear more about this now or at another time?"

When talking about salvation with children, use words and phrases they understand; never assume they understand a concept just because they can repeat certain words. Avoid symbolic terms ("born again," "ask Jesus to come into your heart," "open your heart," etc.) that will confuse these literal-minded thinkers. (You may also use the evangelism booklet *God Loves You!* which is available from Gospel Light.)

1. **God wants you to become His child. Why do you think He wants you in His family?** (See 1 John 3:1.)

2. **You and I and every person in the world have done wrong things. The Bible word for doing wrong is "sin." What do you think should happen to us when we sin?** (See Romans 6:23.)

3. **God loves you so much that He sent His Son to die on the cross to take the punishment for your sin. Because Jesus never sinned, He is the only One who can take the punishment for your sin. On the third day after Jesus died, God brought Him back to life.** (See 1 Corinthians 15:3-4; 1 John 4:14.)

4. **Are you sorry for your sin? Tell God that you are. Do you believe Jesus died for your sin and then rose again? Tell Him that, too. If you tell God you are sorry for your sin and believe that Jesus died to take your sin away, God forgives you.** (See 1 John 1:9.)

5. **The Bible says that when you believe that Jesus is God's Son and that He is alive today, you receive God's gift of eternal life. This gift makes you a child of God. This means God is with you now and forever.** (See John 1:12; 3:16.)

There is great value in encouraging a child to think and pray about what you have said before responding. Encourage the child who makes a decision to become a Christian to tell his or her parents. Give your pastor and the child's Sunday School teacher(s) his or her name. A child's initial response to Jesus is just the beginning of a lifelong process of growing in the faith, so children who make decisions need to be followed up to help them grow. The discipling booklet *Following Jesus* (available from Gospel Light) is an effective tool to use.

Middler Age-Level Characteristics

PHYSICAL

Children at this level have good large- and small-muscle coordination. The girls are generally ahead of the boys. Children can work diligently for longer periods but can become impatient with delays or their own imperfect abilities.

Teaching Tip: The two Set the Story activities in each lesson provide options for including physical activity in this center.

SOCIAL

Children's desire for status within the peer group becomes more intense. Most children remain shy with strangers and exhibit strong preferences for being with a few close friends. Some children still lack essential social skills needed to make and retain friendships.

Teaching Tip: Look for the child who needs a friend. Sit next to that child and include him or her in what you are doing.

SPIRITUAL

Children are open to sensing the need for God's continuous help and guidance. They can recognize the need for a personal Savior. There may be a desire to become a member of God's family. Children who indicate an awareness of sin and a concern about accepting Jesus as Savior need careful guidance without pressure.

Teaching Tips: Give children opportunities to pray. Talk about the forgiving nature of God. Talk personally with a child who shows interest in trusting the Lord Jesus. Use the *God Loves You!* booklet to explain how to become a Christian.

EMOTIONAL

This is the age of teasing, nicknames, criticism and increased verbal skills to vent anger. By eight years of age, children have developed a sense of fair play and a value system of right and wrong. At nine years of age, children are searching for identity beyond membership in the family unit.

Teaching Tips: You have a great opportunity to be a Christian example at a time when children are eagerly searching for models! Encourage children's creativity and boost their self-concept. Let children know by your words and by your actions that "love is spoken here" and that you will not let others hurt them or let them hurt others.

COGNITIVE

Children are beginning to realize there may be valid opinions besides their own. They are becoming able to evaluate alternatives and are less likely than before to fasten onto one viewpoint as the only one possible. Children are also beginning to think in terms of "the whole." Children think more conceptually and have a high level of creativity. By this stage, however, many children have become self-conscious as their understanding has grown to exceed their abilities in some areas.

Teaching Tips: Encourage children to use their Bibles by finding and reading portions of Scripture. Help children understand the meaning of the verses they memorize.

Storytelling Tips

Effective storytelling is a skill that anyone can develop by practicing a few simple principles.

Preparing to Tell the Bible Story

- **Read the story again from God's Word**, even though you may have read the story many times. Use a current Bible translation.
- **Read the story in this book.** This version has been written in words children understand. Know your story well. By telling rather than reading the story, you will be better able to express enthusiasm through your face and voice.
- **Emphasize the key Bible point.** No matter how skillfully you tell a Bible story, it will have little impact unless the point of the story is clear to you and your class. Read the first Bible Aim to find out the key Bible truth emphasized in the story. To make sure this point does not get lost, tell the story so that the point is the focus. As a general rule, the longer the story becomes, the harder it is to keep it focused. Therefore, keep your story brief (approximately one minute per year of the child).
- **Prepare the visual resources and/or props for the Bible story.** These teaching aids will reinforce your words. You may choose to use additional visuals, such as Bible-times costumes for storytellers.
- **Practice telling the story.** Tell it to someone in your family, to a video or audio recorder or to yourself in the mirror. If you feel it is necessary to use notes, write them on a small card and place it in your Bible. Know the story well enough so that you can look directly at the children most of the time with only an occasional glance at your notes.

Telling the Bible Story

- **Teach from the Bible.** Have your open Bible in front of you throughout the story and clearly state that the story is true. Children need to see you as a teacher of God's Word—not merely a reader of a curriculum product.
- **Capture interest at the start.** The best way to begin most stories with children is through an experience interesting to everyone in the group. This experience needs to connect to some aspect of the story. The younger your children, the more crucial it is to start a story with a reference to something in their own experience.
- **Create interest in the story with your voice.**
  1. Try talking a little slower—or faster—to make parts of the story more dramatic.
  2. When the suspense builds, talk softer. A whisper is the most dramatic sound that the human voice can make.
  3. On rare occasions, talk louder—but be considerate of other classes when you do.
- **Create interest in the story with facial expressions.**
  1. Make a conscious effort to smile as you talk.
  2. Try matching your expression to the emotion of a story character.
  3. Work at maintaining eye contact throughout the story. Know your story well enough that you can glance at your Bible and your notes and then look up.
- **Create interest in the story with gestures.**
  1. When you really want attention, gesture with your hands to invite the class to lean in closer to hear what you are saying.
  2. Move closer to a child whose attention is wandering.
- **Be sure to end the story.** Summarize the main point of the story as your closing sentence and then stop! Conclude the story before the children lose interest.

God Gives Us Jesus

SCRIPTURE
Matthew 1:18-25; 3:1-17; 4:23-25; Luke 1:11-60; 2:1-20

BIBLE MEMORY VERSE
This is how God showed his love among us: He sent his one and only Son into the world that we might live through him. 1 John 4:9

LESSON FOCUS
God's love is shown in Jesus.

BIBLE AIMS
During this session, each student may
1. DISCOVER that God sent His Son, Jesus, to show His love for us;
2. DESCRIBE situations in which to show God's love to others;
3. ASK God for help to show His love to others;
4. PRAY to become a member of God's family, as the Holy Spirit leads.

TEACHER'S DEVOTIONAL
"Nothin' says lovin' like somethin' from the oven!" Or at least that's what an old advertising jingle would have you believe. But the advertiser was selling a prepared product and implying that your family would never notice the difference between it and something made from scratch. A baked expression of love could be easy and convenient or it could be difficult and inconvenient, involving time and fresh ingredients! The advertiser would have us believe that the effort required by both methods was the same.

As you might suspect, what people think about love can be a lot like that advertiser's message: Love should be easy and convenient. It should just happen, like a chemical reaction. But what is God's definition of love? First John 3:16 tells us, "This is how we know what love is: Jesus Christ laid down his life for us." When Jesus surrendered His life for us, He did not do what was easy or convenient. Jesus showed us *agape* love—total and complete.

Before your week of VBS work begins, take time to consider your definition of love. How closely does it align with Jesus' definition? Then commit yourself to do cheerfully the work that will be needed—whether easy or difficult, convenient or inconvenient. Ask God to help you show His love, especially during trying moments. God has put you in this place, this week, to help children learn to know what His love really is!

1. Set the Story (5-10 minutes)

If you only have 25 minutes for this center, omit Set the Story.

OPTION A: COCONUT CONNECTIONS

PREPARATION: Photocopy Coconut Cards and cut apart. Place cards in paper bag.

PROCEDURE: Students sit on floor in a circle. They pass coconut around the circle, saying their names as the coconut comes to them. **Remember to whom you passed the coconut, because now we're going to switch places. But you'll always pass the coconut to the same person!**

Students stand up and form a new circle, mixing up their order. Place bag of cards in center of circle. Play "Treasure Forever" from CD as students pass coconut to each other in the same order as in the introductory round. After a few moments, stop the music. The student holding the coconut when music stops selects a Coconut Card from the bag, answers the question and places card back in the bag.

Begin a new round of play. If at the end of a round, the student holding the coconut has already selected a card, he or she selects a student who hasn't had a turn to select a card.

Every few rounds, students stand up and mix up their circle. Continue game as time allows or until all students have had an opportunity to select and answer a question from a card.

KEY CONVERSATION: Who is someone you've met for the first time today? Volunteers respond. **This game helped us meet new people and find out more about them. Sometimes even our best friends don't know everything about us. But today we're going to talk about someone who DOES know everything about us—all the good things and all the bad things we've ever done. And even so, He loves us more than any other friend could! He loves us so much that He sent His own Son, Jesus, to be our Savior.**

OPTION B: LIMBER LIMBO

PREPARATION: Photocopy Limbo Cards, making sure there is at least one card for each student. Cut cards apart and place facedown in a pile on the floor.

PROCEDURE: Ask two students to each hold one end of the broomstick a few feet from card pile. Students hold broomstick about 4 feet (1.2 m) high. Play "The Savior of the World" from CD. Students take turns saying their names while leaning backward to walk under broomstick. Then they walk to card pile and take the top card. Last student to pass under the broomstick selects another student to help hold the broomstick as the two original volunteers each take a turn to go under the broomstick and pick up a card. Any remaining cards in pile can be distributed among pairs of students.

When each student has a card, he or she searches for the student whose card completes the picture and phrase on his or her card. Pairs then work with the rest of the class to put the cards together to complete the verse. (Optional: If cards are not to be reused, partners may tape cards together.) As needed, students use Bible to place the verse cards in the correct order. (Optional: For each additional round, students move under the broomstick in a different fashion [hopping, walking backward, crawling, etc.]. Or lower the broomstick for each round, inviting children to walk underneath without touching the floor with their hands.)

KEY CONVERSATION: What does this verse tell us about Jesus? (That He is God's one and only Son. That He came to Earth.) **What does this verse tell us about God?** (That He sent His Son to show His love for us.) **Today we're going to talk about the extraordinary way that God showed His love for us. And we'll talk about some ways that we can respond to that extraordinary love.**

Materials Checklist

♦ Bible

♦ SonTreasure Island CD and player

♦ Limbo Cards (p. 42)

♦ scissors or paper cutter

♦ broomstick

Optional—

♦ transparent tape

2. Tell the Story (10 minutes)

PREPARATION: Display Session 1 Bible Story Poster. Use Post-it Notes to mark Matthew 1, Matthew 3 and Luke 2 in students' Bibles.

STORYTELLING TIP: Teach from the Bible, not your curriculum. Students need to see you as a teacher of God's Word—not merely a reader of a curriculum product. Have your Bible open in front of you throughout the story and clearly state that the story is true: "This story happened to real people!"

GOD GIVES US JESUS

Matthew 1:18-25; 3:1-17; 4:23-25; Luke 1:11-60; 2:1-20

Introduction

Today I brought a special treasure to show you. (Remove treasure from bag or box. Briefly explain why the object is important to you.) **Who would like to tell us about a special treasure of yours?** Volunteers respond. **The Bible tells us about a special treasure that God gave us—the most valuable treasure ever!** (Optional: Invite students familiar with this story to tell story details. Supplement as needed, referring students to Bible Story Poster for help.)

Angels Tell About Two Babies

A long time ago, God promised that He would send a great Savior into the world. This Savior would forgive people for the wrong things they do and make it possible to be members of God's family. But HUNDREDS of years passed, and the Savior hadn't come!

Then one day God sent an angel to a man named Zechariah. Zechariah and his wife were old and had no children. But the angel told Zechariah that he and his wife Elizabeth would have a baby. The angel also said to name the baby John. The angel described the job God had for John to do when he grew up. John would help people get ready for the promised Savior.

Months later, when Elizabeth was pregnant, she received a visit from her cousin Mary. As Mary approached, the baby inside Elizabeth's womb jumped for joy! Mary told Elizabeth that she had been visited by an angel, just like Zechariah! The angel told Mary she was going to have a baby—God's Son. Her baby would be Jesus, the Savior God had promised.

Mary told the angel's message to Joseph, the man she was going to marry. Then an angel also came to visit Joseph. The angel told Joseph about this special baby. **Let's read Matthew 1:21 to hear what the angel told Joseph.**

The Babies Are Born

When John was born to Zechariah and Elizabeth, all their neighbors and relatives were happy for them.

But when it came time for Mary's baby to be born, she and Joseph had to take a long trip. Because the ruler of all the countries in that part of the world wanted to know who he could tax, all the men had to return to the towns their families had come from. Joseph and Mary went to Bethlehem because Joseph belonged to the family of King David from long, long ago.

It was terribly crowded in Bethlehem. The only place Mary and Joseph could find to stay was a stable for animals. It wasn't very fancy, but it was warm and better than being outside. **How do you think Joseph and Mary must have felt that night in the stable?**

Materials Checklist

- Session 1 Bible Story Poster from Elementary Teaching Resources
- Post-it Notes
- bag or box containing a personal treasure (signed baseball, bronzed baby shoes, favorite book, heirloom jewelry or watch, etc.)

For each student and teacher—
- Bible

Teaching Tip

For a fun alternative or supplement to this or any Bible story in this course, ask teachers, helpers or student volunteers to perform the Bible story skits found in the *Assemblies & Skits Production Guide.*

That night God's one and only Son was born. Joseph and Mary named Him Jesus. Mary wrapped baby Jesus in cloths and laid Him down to sleep on hay in an animal feed box, called a manger.

That same night, shepherds were nearby in the fields with their sheep. Suddenly an angel came to them. The bright light of God's glory was shining all around! The shepherds were afraid. But the angel said not to be afraid. There was good news: The Savior, Christ the Lord, was born! **Let's read Luke 2:10-12 and find out what else the angel said.** A great crowd of angels appeared in the sky, praising God. The shepherds were amazed!

After the angels went back to heaven, the shepherds hurried off and found the baby Jesus. They worshiped Him and then told everyone they met about the wonderful baby! Then the shepherds returned to their sheep in the fields, praising God.

The Babies Grow Up

When Zechariah and Elizabeth's son, John, grew up, he lived away from the towns, out in the desert. John told people the important message God had given him. He told people how to get ready for the Savior God had promised. John told people that they needed to admit the wrong things they were doing. They needed to stop doing wrong things and begin doing what is right.

Many people admitted they had done wrong and asked God to forgive their sins. John led them into the Jordan River and baptized them with water. Baptism showed that they wanted to obey God. John baptized so many people that he was called "John the Baptist."

One day, as John was baptizing people at the river, he looked up and saw Jesus coming.

"John," Jesus said, "I want you to baptize Me." Jesus' request must have surprised John, because he knew that Jesus had never done or said ANYTHING wrong. Jesus didn't have any sins to be sorry for!

"No, Jesus!" John said. "It is You who should baptize me!"

But Jesus insisted on being baptized. He wanted to show He was willing to follow God in everything He did. So John baptized Jesus.

As soon as Jesus came out of the water, something amazing happened! **Let's read Matthew 3:17 to find out what happened. What do you think the people at the river thought when they heard the voice?** That voice was from God. God wanted everyone to know that Jesus is His Son—the Savior He had promised them so long ago.

Conclusion

God showed His love to us by giving His one and only Son, Jesus, to live among us. Because God loves us so much, every day there are times we can show His love to others. Learning about God's love is like discovering a treasure. This week at SonTreasure Island, you'll find out more about the treasure of God's love and the many ways Jesus showed God's love to us.

Focus on Evangelism

Because He loves us, God wants us to be a part of His family forever. When you believe that Jesus is God's Son, admit the wrong things you do and trust Jesus to forgive you, you can become a member of God's family.

Invite students interested in knowing more about becoming members of God's family to talk with you or another teacher after class. (See "Leading a Child to Christ," p. 8.)

3. Apply the Story (10-15 minutes)

Materials Checklist

◆ colored markers

For each student—

◆ Session 1 Treasure Guide page

Optional—

◆ SonTreasure Gem Stickers

BIBLE STORY REVIEW

To review Bible story, students complete "God Gives Us Jesus" activity on Session 1 page. **In our story today, why didn't John the Baptist think he should baptize Jesus?** (Because Jesus had never done anything wrong. Jesus had no sins to be sorry for!) **Why did Jesus want to be baptized?** (He wanted to show He was willing to follow God in everything He did.) **What special thing happened when Jesus was baptized?** (God spoke, saying that Jesus was His Son and that He was pleased with Him.)

Indicate the Daily Treasure logo on the page. **Each day at SonTreasure Island, we'll discover a new Daily Treasure—something the Bible teaches us about God's love. Today's Daily Treasure reminds us that "God's Love Is Giving"—and because God loves us, He gave us the greatest treasure of all: Jesus!**

MEMORY VERSE/APPLICATION

Students turn Session 1 page over. Divide class into three groups. Lead first group to say, "This is how God showed his love among us." Lead second group to say, "He sent his one and only Son into the world." Lead third group to say, "That we might live through him." (Optional: Give each student a SonTreasure Gem Sticker to place next to the memory verse.) **For whom did God send His Son into the world?** (Everyone. All the people in the world.) **Our verse says that we can live through Jesus. What do you think that means?** Students respond. **It means that Jesus made a way for us to be members of God's family and live forever. Jesus is the Savior God had promised to send!**

Students complete "Giving God's Love" activity. **Every day we have opportunities to show God's love to others, even when we don't want to or when others aren't showing love to us.**

PRAYER

When are some times that it might be hard to show God's love? (When someone is unkind. When feeling tired. When a little brother or sister is being a pest.) **Even when it's hard to show God's love, if we ask Him, God will help us. Let's pray.** Lead students in prayer, inviting volunteers to ask God for His help to show love to others.

Jesus Helps a Young Girl and a Sick Woman

GOD'S LOVE IS KIND

SCRIPTURE
Matthew 9:18-26; Mark 5:21-43; Luke 8:40-56

BIBLE MEMORY VERSE
Love is patient, love is kind. It does not envy, it does not boast, it is not proud.
1 Corinthians 13:4

LESSON FOCUS
God's love is kind and patient.

BIBLE AIMS
During this session, each student may
1. DISCOVER that Jesus showed God's love by healing a young girl and a sick woman;
2. IDENTIFY kind and patient actions that show concern for others and their problems;
3. ASK God to help him or her show kind and patient actions in specific situations;
4. PRAY to become a member of God's family, as the Holy Spirit leads.

TEACHER'S DEVOTIONAL
Late-afternoon checkout lines at grocery stores can reveal a lot about human character. Amid beeping machines and wailing toddlers, you might hear "That doesn't look like fewer than 10 items!" or "Why do I always get behind someone with coupons?" or "Why doesn't she make that child hush?" Even if we consider ourselves too kind to actually say such things aloud, we often think them, or maybe we throw a dirty look or two—filled with rising irritation at the thoughtlessness of others!

In contrast, love in action is patient and kind. It behaves with humility and doesn't focus exclusively on personal agendas or achievements. Love expressed through patience is not so much about waiting as about being fully present where we are, in the present moment. Living expectantly in the here and now reminds us that God has placed us in situations He has designed for us. Ephesians 2:10 tells us, "For we are God's workmanship, created in Christ Jesus to do good works, which God prepared in advance for us to do."

Trusting God's design for every moment of our lives means that we can practice love in every difficult situation. We can pray for those who tax our patience, trusting that God's love and kindness can prevail in every circumstance. As you work with God's children this week, find ways to share the treasure of God's love, even in the most difficult moments.

1. Set the Story (5-10 minutes)

If you only have 25 minutes for this center, omit Set the Story.

OPTION A: SWELL SHELLS

PREPARATION: Place six seashells on a paper plate. Place an empty plate next to plate of shells. Set up similar plates for each pair of students, allowing several feet of space between each setup.

PROCEDURE: Students divide into pairs. Each pair stands by a set of paper plates. After taking off their shoes and socks, partners race to move all the shells from one paper plate to the other, using only their feet.
Students may work separately or together.
As each pair finishes, announce their time. Play additional rounds, challenging students to beat the best previous time.

KEY CONVERSATION: What was difficult about this game? What would have made moving the shells easier? When are some times you had to be patient while playing today's game? It would have taken a lot longer to move the shells if you didn't have a partner to help you. Helping each other is one way we can show God's love. Today we'll talk about different ways we can show God's love by helping others and caring about their problems.

OPTION B: PINEAPPLE PICK

PREPARATION: For each team, photocopy a set of Pineapple Cards. Cut apart and tape each one onto a separate yellow plate. Place yellow plates and plates of other colors in bag to fill it. Place bags several feet apart in playing area.

PROCEDURE: Students divide into teams of three or four members and line up behind the starting line. Hold up a plate. **Let's pretend these plates are tropical fruits. Somewhere in each bag are some yellow pineapples. On each pineapple is part of an important message—but you'll have to put the pineapples in order to discover the message!** At your signal, first player on each team runs to team's bag and searches for a yellow plate. Then player brings the plate back to his or her team and next player on team runs to bag. When the team has collected all six plates, team members place plates in verse order, using Bible as needed. Students read verse aloud.

KEY CONVERSATION: When might it be hard to be patient and kind? Who are some people that it can be hard to be patient with? One way we can show patience and kindness is by caring about others and their problems. When we care about others, we're being patient and kind, just as our verse tells us to do. Caring about the problems of others is a great way to show God's love!

Materials Checklist

- Pineapple Cards (p. 43)
- scissors or paper cutter
- masking tape

For each team of 3 or 4 students—

- Bible
- small paper plates in a variety of colors, including six yellow plates
- large bag

2. Tell the Story (10 minutes)

Materials Checklist

♦ Session 2 Bible Story Poster from Elementary Teaching Resources

♦ Post-it Notes

For each student and teacher—

♦ Bible

PREPARATION: Display Session 2 Bible Story Poster. Use Post-it Notes to mark Mark 5 in students' Bibles.

STORYTELLING TIP: Know your story well enough to talk with your students rather than read to them. Use a highlighter to mark key facts. By telling, rather than reading the story, you will be better able to express enthusiasm through your face and voice and better able to use your hands to hold objects such as the signs suggested for use in today's Bible Storytelling Option.

JESUS HELPS A YOUNG GIRL AND A SICK WOMAN

Matthew 9:18-26; Mark 5:21-43; Luke 8:40-56

Introduction

When have you been in a large crowd? What would you do if you needed to get to the front of a crowd quickly? Volunteers tell ideas. **Today in our story we are going to hear about a man who was in a hurry to get to the front of a big crowd.**

A Man in Need

"Did you hear that Jesus is back in town?" The news spread from house to house. Soon a giant crowd gathered to see and hear Jesus. Some of the people wanted to see what Jesus would do and hear what He would say. Others wanted Jesus to heal them or help them with their problems. Still others just wanted to be close to Him. **Why might you have wanted to see Jesus?**

A man named Jairus (JI-ruhs) was so VERY anxious to see Jesus that he pushed through the crowd. People respectfully moved out of the way so that he could get close to Jesus. You see, Jairus was an important man. He was in charge of the synagogue in town. And people could see he really wanted to get close to Jesus! **Read Mark 5:22-23 to find out what Jairus did.** Jairus loved his daughter. Jesus cared about Jairus and his daughter, too. So Jesus went with Jairus right away.

As Jesus, His friends and Jairus tried to hurry through the huge crowd, people kept pushing in all around them. It was hard to even move! Suddenly, Jesus stopped and asked, "Who touched Me?"

"Who touched You?" Jesus' friends asked. "Well, everyone did! We are all being trampled by this crowd!" But this touch had been different. And Jesus knew it.

A Woman of Faith

Someone had touched Jesus' clothes for a specific reason. And Jesus knew that His power had healed someone. Jesus kept looking, waiting patiently for the person to step forward. Finally a woman came up, trembling with fear. **Read Mark 5:25-26 to find out who this woman was.** The woman told Jesus, "I have been sick for a very long time. I knew that if I could just touch Your clothes, I would be healed—and I am!" **What do you suppose the people in the crowd must have thought about the woman?**

Jesus smiled and told the woman, "Your faith has healed you. Go in peace. You won't suffer anymore."

Just then some men came pushing through the crowd with terrible news. "Don't bother Jesus anymore," they told Jairus. "Your daughter is already dead."

Oh, no! Jairus must have thought. *If this crowd hadn't been in the way—or if that woman hadn't stopped Jesus—we could have gotten to my daughter in time!*

Jesus told Jairus, "Don't be afraid; just believe." So Jesus and Jairus and the others continued through the crowd to Jairus's house. When they finally arrived there, ANOTHER crowd was gathering outside—a funeral crowd! Many people had come to the house to mourn for the girl. They were wailing and crying and making all kinds of noise. **Read what Jesus said to this crowd in Mark 5:39.**

What Jesus meant was that He was going to bring the girl back to life. But the people didn't understand. They laughed at Jesus' words. They had seen the girl. She was dead! They'd never heard of someone being healed from death!

Jesus sent them all out of the house. Then Jesus took Peter, James, John, and Jairus and his wife into the room where the girl's body lay.

Bible Storytelling Option

Before class, print in large letters on a separate sheet of construction paper each of these phrases: "Hooray!" "Oh, no!" and "Gasp!" Divide the class into three teams. Assign each team to a sign. Before telling the story, hold up each sign and practice saying "Hoo-ray!" "Oh, no!" and making a gasping sound with the appropriate team.

Instruct teams to say what is written on their signs when you hold them up at appropriate times in the story. For example, use "Hooray!" when Jesus agrees to go with Jairus, "Gasp!" when Jesus says that He felt someone touch Him, and "Oh, no!" when friends announce that the girl has died.

A Healthy Girl

Jesus took the girl's hand in His own and said, "Little girl, get up." And right away, the little girl opened her eyes. She sat up! Then she began to walk around! Jairus and his wife and Jesus' friends were amazed! The girl really had been dead; but now, because of Jesus' words, she was ALIVE and completely well! Jesus showed that His love and power are so great that He can care for people in all kinds of situations!

Conclusion

Just as Jesus was kind to the people in our story, so Jesus is kind and helps us. Just as Jesus was patient and didn't get angry with the crowds or the woman who touched his robe, so Jesus is patient with us. Knowing that God's love is kind and patient is one of the treasures we can discover this week at SonTreasure Island. Every day there are times we can show God's love by being kind and patient with others. It all starts with caring about others and their problems.

God loves us and wants to help us be kind and patient. As members of God's family, we can ask for His help! Invite children interested in knowing more about becoming members of God's family to talk with you or another teacher after class. (See "Leading a Child to Christ," p. 8.)

3. Apply the Story (10-15 minutes)

Materials Checklist

◆ colored markers

For each student—

◆ Session 2 Treasure Guide page

Optional—

◆ SonTreasure Gem Stickers

BIBLE STORY REVIEW

To review Bible story, students complete "Jesus Helps a Young Girl and a Sick Woman" activity on Session 2 page. **What did Jesus do in today's story that showed He was patient?** (Spent time with the crowds of people. Followed Jairus to his home. Stopped to help the woman who touched Him.) **What kind actions did Jesus show in today's story?** (He healed the woman. He healed the girl.) **Jesus didn't just TALK about God's love— He lived it! Jesus' kind and patient actions were real-life examples of God's love.**

Indicate the Daily Treasure logo on the page. **Today's Daily Treasure reminds us that "God's Love Is Kind"—and He wants US to use kind and patient actions to show His love to others.**

MEMORY VERSE/APPLICATION

Students turn Session 2 page over. Lead students in saying the verse, clapping once for each syllable of the verse. If time permits, repeat verse several times, asking students to suggest other rhythmic motions (snap fingers, stomp feet, etc.). (Optional: Give each student a SonTreasure Gem Sticker to place next to the memory verse.) **We all know what it means to be patient and kind. We also know what it means to be proud. But what does our verse mean when it talks about envy?** (To want what somebody else has for yourself.) **What does it mean to boast?** (To brag about how good you are or the things that you have.)

When we are kind and patient, we won't act proud, envious or boastful. We will show God's love by caring about others and their problems. What are some ways you can show you care about someone else's problems? (Share food with people in a homeless shelter. Donate clothes to a missions project. Invite someone to go to church. Help someone with his or her homework or chores. Be kind to someone new or who is being left out.)

Students complete "Colorful Gems" activity. **It isn't always easy to be kind and patient. We don't always want to show love or help someone. And sometimes it can seem like a real pain to have to share. But God has done all these things for us because He loves us! And we can show God's love to others, even when it isn't easy.**

PRAYER

Because He loves us, God promises to always help us. Even though it isn't always easy to care about others and their problems, God promises to help us when we ask. What is a way that you can show God's love this week? Volunteers respond. Pray, asking God to help each student do what he or she wrote. Conclude by asking God to show us ways we can demonstrate His love by being kind and patient and caring about others and their problems.

MIDDLER ♦ SESSION THREE

Jesus Cares for a Samaritan Woman

SCRIPTURE
John 4:1-42

BIBLE MEMORY VERSE
[Love] is not rude, it is not self-seeking. 1 Corinthians 13:5

LESSON FOCUS
God's love is for everyone.

BIBLE AIMS
During this session, each student may
1. DISCOVER that Jesus showed God's love to a Samaritan woman whom others might have ignored;
2. IDENTIFY situations in which it might be hard to show God's love;
3. ASK God to help him or her show God's love to people whom others may not care about;
4. PRAY to become a member of God's family, as the Holy Spirit leads.

TEACHER'S DEVOTIONAL
The car that just cut you off has a bumper sticker that reads, "It's all about ME!" More than ever, people seem to accept rude, selfish behavior as acceptable, perhaps even desirable. The current thinking seems to hold that it's okay to show love to others, but the most important thing is to love yourself first.

What does authentic love, God's love, teach us about dealing with others? Considering another person first—regardless of power, popularity or position—expresses love free from rudeness and self-seeking. God's love for us is the only real basis for our personal dignity or worth. Contrast Jesus' words to the outcast, derided Samaritan woman with the ways pagan cultures treat their weak, poor or outcast. Only God's love and grace give us the ability to show others kind behavior, gracious words and unselfish deeds.

Compassion and consideration for others is a natural outgrowth of receiving God's unconditional love in Christ. Only forgiven hearts produce genuinely loving actions and attitudes. When we show grace to another, instead of being rude or self-seeking, our actions acknowledge that we have received God's grace. It also gives both example and permission to the forgiven one to show grace to another. A worldwide revolution in true love begins right here, right now—as we show God's love to the children in our classes, our VBS coworkers and the other people we encounter in our everyday lives.

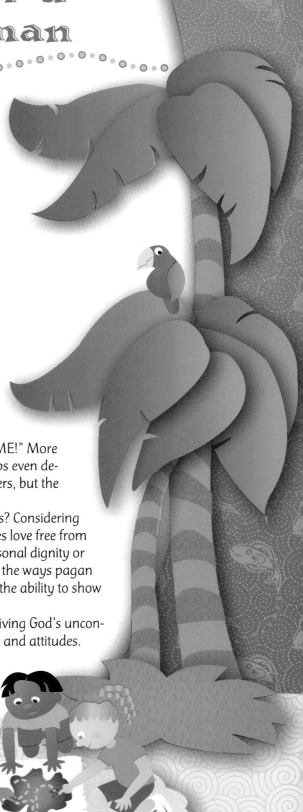

1. Set the Story (5-10 minutes)

If you only have 25 minutes for this center, omit Set the Story.

OPTION A: LIFESAVER PASS

Materials Checklist

♦ SonTreasure Island CD and player

For each student—

♦ toothpick

♦ 1 Lifesavers® candy

PROCEDURE: Play "God's Love Is for You" from CD. Give each student a toothpick. Students form a circle and use toothpicks to pass a Lifesavers® candy around the circle. Give the last student holding the candy when the music stops another candy to eat. He or she then starts the next round with the original candy. Continue until each student receives a candy, or if time is limited, offer a candy to anyone who has not received one.

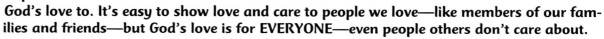

KEY CONVERSATION: Making sure that everyone gets a treat is a way to show God's love. What are some other ways to show God's love? (Be kind and patient. Tell them God loves them. Help them.) **These are all good ways to show God's love. Now that we know HOW to show God's love, it's important to know WHO we can show** God's love to. It's easy to show love and care to people we love—like members of our families and friends—but God's love is for EVERYONE—even people others don't care about.

OPTION B: FISH TOSS

PREPARATION: Photocopy a set of Fish Cards onto card stock for each team of three or four students. Cut out cards. To weight cards, place a large paper clip at the top of each card. Keep cards in sets. Place containers at one end of playing area, several feet apart. Make a masking-tape line approximately 4 feet (1.2 m) in front of each container.

PROCEDURE: Each team of three or four members forms a line behind a masking-tape line. Give a set of Fish Cards to the first student in each line. At your signal, students try to toss the cards into their team's container. When a student has tossed all of the cards, he or she retrieves the cards that did not end up in container, hands them to the next student in line and goes to the end of the line. Teams continue until all of their cards are in their container.

Team members then race to put the verse cards in order and read the verse aloud. Repeat game as time permits.

TABLE-TOP ALTERNATIVE: For each team of four, make four copies of Fish Cards, cut apart and mix cards together. Teams play a game like "Go Fish," asking for cards by the words on the cards.

KEY CONVERSATION: We had to take turns while playing our game. What is hard about waiting to take a turn? Volunteers respond. **Sometimes we get so excited it's hard to wait! Or sometimes we think we can do a better job than someone else and so we want to take over and do it for him or her. But our verse today says that love is not rude or self-seeking. What do you think "self-seeking" means?** Letting other people take their turn is the opposite of being self-seeking! Someone who is not self-seeking takes time to show God's love to others, no matter who they are and no matter what the situation is.

Materials Checklist

- Fish Cards (p. 44)
- card stock
- scissors or paper cutter
- large paper clips
- masking tape
- measuring stick

For each team of 3 or 4 students—

- container (treasure chest, cardboard box, wastebasket, etc.)

2. Tell the Story (10 minutes)

Materials Checklist

- Session 3 Bible Story Poster from *Elementary Teaching Resources*
- Post-it Notes

For each student and teacher—
- Bible

PREPARATION: Display the Session 3 Bible Story Poster. Use Post-it Notes to mark John 4 in students' Bibles.

STORYTELLING TIP: Use the conversation suggested in the Introduction and Conclusion. The question in the Introduction is designed to hook students' attention by relating the story to something with which each student can personally relate. The Conclusion sums up the story action and applies it to the focus for each session as well as the life of each student.

JESUS CARES FOR A SAMARITAN WOMAN John 4:1-42

Introduction

Sometimes people can surprise us. (Share an example of a time when someone said or did something kind that you didn't expect.) **Have you ever thought you knew exactly what someone would say or do, but then they said or did something completely different?** Volunteers respond. **Today we will hear about a woman who was surprised by something Jesus said and did.**

A Sunny Day

Jesus and His friends traveled many places to tell people about God's love. One day, the sun was shining brightly as Jesus and His friends walked on a road through the country of Samaria. Now most Jewish people in Jesus' time would not go NEAR Samaria. You see, Jews and Samaritans had disliked each other for HUNDREDS of years. But that didn't stop Jesus from visiting Samaria. He had important work to do!

It was around noon. Jesus and His friends were tired of walking and were very hot. When they came to a town, Jesus rested by the well just outside of town. **Read John 4:8 to find out where Jesus' friends went.**

A Thirsty Woman

At that time, most water came from wells dug deep into the ground, so travelers usually carried small buckets to lower into wells to get water. The disciples must have taken the bucket with them, because Jesus had no way to get water.

Pretty soon, a woman came toward Him carrying a big jar to get water. When she set down her jar, Jesus asked her for a drink of water. The woman was VERY surprised! She wondered why Jesus talked to her AT ALL. You see, in Bible times, a man and a woman did not speak to each other if they met on the street. And Jews and Samaritans usually NEVER talked to each other!

A Living Water

Read John 4:10 to find out what Jesus said to the woman. How do you think the woman felt when Jesus spoke to her? The woman didn't understand. "How can You give me water?" she asked. "You don't have a bucket or a rope. And this well is VERY deep. Where would You get this living water?"

"Anyone who drinks water from this well will become thirsty again," Jesus said. "But whoever drinks the water I give will NEVER be thirsty again. The water I give is like a flowing stream inside a person. It will last forever!"

The woman thought about what Jesus said. "Give me some of this water!" she said. "Then I won't have to come to the well every day for water." She thought Jesus was talking about water she could drink. She didn't understand that Jesus meant He could give her life from God that would last forever.

Then the woman asked Jesus some questions about why the Samaritans worshiped God in one place and why the Jews worshiped God in another place. Jesus told her that the place where people worshiped was not as important as what was in their minds and hearts as they worshiped. He said God wants people to worship Him with their whole hearts, not just pretend to be worshiping Him.

Then Jesus did something REALLY surprising. He told her some things about her that a stranger would never know. He said He knew about her sins—the wrong things she had done. Back then, most people wouldn't have even spoken to a woman who had done so many wrong things. But even though Jesus knew about them, He still took the time to talk to her.

The woman was amazed! Even though she had just met Him, Jesus knew EVERYTHING about her! She said, "I know that when the Savior God promised comes, He will tell us everything."

Read John 4:26 to see how Jesus answered the woman. That was exciting news that people had been waiting hundreds and hundreds of years to hear. And Jesus had told HER, this Samaritan woman, that He was the Savior God had promised to send!

The woman was SO excited that she left her water jug at the well and hurried back to town. "Come and see a man who told me everything I have ever done!" the woman told the people in the town. "Could He be the Savior?" she asked. **What do you think the people did?**

People from the town followed the woman to Jesus. If the Savior had come, they wanted to see Him! Many of them believed that Jesus was the Savior because the woman told them about the things Jesus had done and said! This town in Samaria would never be the same—and it all started because Jesus showed God's love to a woman most people would have expected Him to ignore.

Conclusion

Jesus cared for the Samaritan woman, even though the people in her own town probably avoided her! She was so happy that Jesus accepted her and cared enough to talk with her that she wanted to tell EVERYONE about Him. Showing God's love to all people, even those others don't care about, is like giving them a special treasure.

Focus on Evangelism

Because Jesus cares for us so much, He wants all of us to believe He is the Savior, just as the people in our story did. When we believe that Jesus is God's Son, we can become members of God's family. Invite children interested in knowing more about becoming members of God's family to talk with you or another teacher after class. (See "Leading a Child to Christ," p. 8.)

Bible Storytelling Option

Divide class into three groups. Assign each group a location in the room and an element of the Bible-story setting: the well, the road or the town.

Groups sit together, arranging themselves to form the object or place they were assigned. (Students forming the well clasp hands and stand in a circle. Students forming the road sit in parallel lines. Students forming the town sit in pairs with arms over shoulders to form buildings.) As you tell the story, move from one area to the next, as people in the story travel from place to place.

3. Apply the Story (10-15 minutes)

BIBLE STORY REVIEW

To review Bible story, students complete "Jesus Cares for a Samaritan Woman" activity on Session 3 page. **What people did the Jews usually not talk to?** (Samaritans.) **Who else didn't like the woman?** (The people of the town.) **Why do you think Jesus talked to the Samaritan woman?** (He cared about her and wanted her to know that He could help her.) **What did the woman tell the townspeople?** (That Jesus was the Savior. That He knew everything about her.) **Jesus took time to talk to the woman at the well. His love and care meant so much to her that she told the townspeople all about Him. She and many other people came to believe that Jesus is God's Son—the promised Savior!**

Indicate the Daily Treasure logo on the page. **Today's Daily Treasure reminds us that "God's Love Is Caring." That doesn't just mean** caring about people that others like or people who can help us—God's love means caring about everyone!

MEMORY VERSE/APPLICATION

Students turn Session 3 page over. Point to individual students who each say one word of the verse. (Optional: Give each student a SonTreasure Gem Sticker to place next to the memory verse.) **What does our verse mean when it talks about being "self-seeking"?** (Putting yourself first. Caring about yourself more than others. Always trying to get what you want for yourself.) **When we care for others, we put them before ourselves. What are some ways to put others first?** (Letting someone else go first at the computer. Giving a sister the bigger slice of cake. Holding the door open for someone else to walk through.)

Students complete "Fishy Situations" activity. **It's easy to show God's love to others who are our friends and who are nice to us. But it isn't ALWAYS easy to show God's love to everyone. God will always help us show His love and care to others, even to people you and your friends may not like. All we have to do is ask Him.**

PRAYER

Some people are easier to show God's love to than others. It can be hard to show love to someone who's been mean to us or someone different from us or someone our friends don't like. Tell an age-appropriate example of a time when it was difficult for you to show God's love to someone. **The more we learn about God's love, the easier it is to show His love to others.** Close in prayer, asking God to help us find ways to show His love to everyone.

Jesus Forgives Zacchaeus

SCRIPTURE
Luke 19:1-10

BIBLE MEMORY VERSE
[Love] is not easily angered, it keeps no record of wrongs. Love does not delight in evil but rejoices with the truth. 1 Corinthians 13:5-6

LESSON FOCUS
God's love is forgiving.

BIBLE AIMS
During this session, each student may
1. DISCOVER that Jesus showed God's love by forgiving Zacchaeus, the tax collector;
2. DESCRIBE actions that show forgiveness to others;
3. ASK God to help him or her forgive others;
4. PRAY to become a member of God's family, as the Holy Spirit leads.

TEACHER'S DEVOTIONAL
Some of us are planners. We neatly file all records, regularly balance the books and use spreadsheets to calculate our debts and assets. Zacchaeus, the tax collector, was probably a planner. Judging by his wealth and his neighbors' dislike of him, he was probably very thorough. He may have even kept a neat set of DOUBLE books—one for the Romans and one for himself.

Planners probably also understand Zacchaeus's initial shock when Jesus called him down from the tree and invited Himself to dinner. That appointment was not in Zacchaeus's personal planner—not even in pencil! But in one act and one statement, Jesus lavished Zacchaeus with a love, forgiveness and acceptance that Zacchaeus had never known. It didn't take Zacchaeus long to recover his balance. He realized the great grace he'd received and declared that he was giving back fourfold to anyone he'd cheated!

Whether or not we balance our books and file our receipts, there is one area of accounting in which we can relax: We need never keep any record of wrong! Jesus tells us to stop keeping our own double sets of books—our "Christian" set and another set in which we note in permanent ink unpaid debts. As forgiven followers of Jesus, we are free to forgive all debts, burn the old records and let Him free us from the pain, bitterness and frustration bound up in every one of those old accounts. The forgiveness God lavishes in Jesus' name frees you to focus on giving your students the greatest treasure ever—God's amazing love!

1. Set the Story (5-10 minutes)

If you only have 25 minutes for this center, omit Set the Story.

OPTION A: BUILDING SAND CASTLES

PREPARATION: Photocopy the Sand Castle Patterns onto card stock and cut out. Trace patterns onto sandpaper, construction paper or paper bags to make at least one shape for each student, plus a few extras. Cut out shapes and place in bucket. At the top of the large sheet of paper, print "Kids can forgive others when . . ." and post paper on wall.

PROCEDURE: Students each select a shape from the bucket and write or draw a time when kids may have trouble getting along and need to show forgiveness to others. As students complete shapes, they tape shapes to large sheet of paper, using the shapes to form a sand castle. As time allows, students complete additional shapes.

KEY CONVERSATION: When are some times that kids might get angry at each other? Hurt another person's feelings? Volunteers answer. **It's not always easy to get along with our friends and the people in our families. Today we're going to talk about something that can be really hard to do—being kind to people who have been unkind to us.**

Materials Checklist

- Sand Castle Patterns (pp. 45-46)
- card stock
- scissors
- pencil
- sandpaper, brown construction paper or brown paper bags
- bucket
- large sheet of paper
- colored markers
- masking tape

OPTION B: MUSICAL MAP-WALK

Materials Checklist

♦ Bible
♦ SonTreasure Island CD and player
♦ Map Puzzle (p. 47)
♦ scissors
♦ stopwatch or watch with second hand

PREPARATION: Photocopy Map Puzzle. If you have more than six students, copy as many times as needed to make at least one puzzle piece for each student. Cut out puzzle pieces and place them in a circle on the floor.

PROCEDURE: Students play a game like Cake Walk. Play "If We Turn" from CD as students walk around the circle. After a few moments, stop the music. Students stop and pick up the nearest puzzle piece. Using the Bible as needed, students work together to put the puzzle together. Use a stopwatch or watch to time the round. Once the puzzle is complete, students read the verse together. Play additional rounds as time allows, trying to beat the best previous time.

KEY CONVERSATION: **What do you think "it keeps no record of wrongs" means?** (Not keeping a list of the wrong things people do. Not holding a grudge.) **What do you think would happen if someone held a grudge whenever anyone was unkind to him or her?** (He or she would lose friends. He or she would always be hurt and angry.) **Forgiving someone means letting go of our grudges. God forgives us, and He wants us to show His love by forgiving others, too.**

2. Tell the Story (10 minutes)

PREPARATION: Display Session 4 Bible Story Poster. Use Post-it Notes to mark Luke 19 in students' Bibles.

STORYTELLING TIP: Invite students already familiar with the story to help you tell parts of the Bible story. Be sure to explain the purpose and value of studying Bible stories more than once by saying, **One of the reasons the Bible is such a great book is that as we grow older, we can learn new things about God, even from stories we've heard many times.** Challenge students to listen to hear if they can learn something new about Jesus.

JESUS FORGIVES ZACCHAEUS Luke 19:1-10

Introduction

When have you seen someone cheat or treat others unfairly? Today we'll find out how a man cheated others so that he could become rich. Listen to hear what happened when this man met Jesus.

Tax Time

When Jesus lived on Earth, the people in Israel had to pay taxes to the Romans. The Israelites weren't happy about paying this money. First of all, they didn't LIKE the Romans. And second of all, paying taxes to Rome took money that the Israelites needed to buy food and clothes. And WORST of all, every time they paid money to the Romans, it reminded the Israelites of how unhappy they were that the Romans were in charge at all!

But one man WAS happy about people paying money to Rome. This man was the tax collector. His name was Zacchaeus. Not only was he a tax collector, but he was also RICH. He had a big house and nice clothes. But he had NO friends.

Zacchaeus was rich because he took more money from people than they were supposed to pay in taxes. Then Zacchaeus kept the extra money for himself! Everyone in town could see that he had extra money because of his fancy house and his expensive clothes. NO one liked him!

A Leafy Lift

But one day Jesus came to the town where Zacchaeus lived. People crowded along the road, waiting to see Jesus. They had heard many good things about Jesus. The news of Jesus as a teacher of God's Word had spread throughout the country. They had also heard Jesus was kind and could heal people who were sick. Everyone was excited to see this man they had heard so much about!

Zacchaeus wanted to see Jesus, too. But he couldn't. **Read Luke 19:3 to find out why Zacchaeus couldn't see Jesus.** And nobody would let him through the crowd! He couldn't see Jesus at all!

Zacchaeus REALLY wanted to see Jesus. He had probably heard many wonderful things about Jesus. So he ran past the crowd. He could see a big tree up ahead! Quickly Zacchaeus climbed up the tree. NOW he could see! He could see Jesus—coming closer and closer!

When Jesus was right under the tree where Zacchaeus was sitting, Zacchaeus got a big surprise. Jesus looked up right at him! Then he got another surprise! Jesus spoke to him. **Read Luke 19:5 to find out what Jesus said to Zacchaeus.**

Well, the people sure knew about the bad things Zacchaeus had done. And now here was Jesus wanting to visit him! **How do you think the people felt about that?** The crowd was surprised that Jesus would want to be with that greedy, cheating tax collector! They must have wondered, *Why would Jesus want to be friends with a man like that?* But Jesus did! And Jesus' love CHANGED Zacchaeus.

A Changed Man

Zacchaeus said, "I want to give half of everything I have to poor people. And if I have cheated anyone, I will give back FOUR TIMES as much money as I took!" **Why do you think Zacchaeus wanted to give money away now?** Zacchaeus wanted EVERYONE to know that he was different now. He wanted to give, not take!

Jesus knew that Zacchaeus was sorry for cheating and stealing and doing other wrong things. Jesus forgave Zacchaeus. And Zacchaeus must have been VERY glad Jesus had forgiven him!

Conclusion

Zacchaeus thought that because he'd lied and cheated people, Jesus would never care for him. But Zacchaeus discovered a very important treasure. Through Jesus, he discovered that God loved and forgave him. Sometimes we may feel that because we've done something wrong, God doesn't care for us. But just like He forgave Zacchaeus, God will forgive us for the wrong things we do, too. All we have to do is be truly sorry for what we have done and ask Him to forgive us.

Each one of us has done things that are wrong. But the good news is that God sent His Son, Jesus, to take the punishment for your sins and my sins. If we truly want Him to forgive us, He will. Invite children interested in knowing more about becoming members of God's family to talk with you or another teacher after class. (See "Leading a Child to Christ," p. 8.)

(See "Leading a Child to Christ," p. 8.)

Bible Storytelling Option

Before telling the story, practice the following motions and Spanish words with children. (Note: You can simplify this activity by just using the motions and not the words.)

Spanish is one of the languages spoken in the Caribbean Islands. We're going to learn some Spanish words! Whenever you hear me say the words "money" or "rich," rub the fingers of one hand with the thumb and say "dinero" (dee-NEH-roh). When I say "crowd" or "people," put your arm around the person sitting next to you and say "gente" (hehn-TAY). For the word "tree," raise your hands and sway from side to side, saying "árbol" (AHR-bohl). Pause after each instruction for children to practice motion and Spanish word.

3. Apply the Story (10-15 minutes)

Materials Checklist

♦ colored markers

For each student—
♦ Session 4 Treasure Guide page

Optional—
♦ SonTreasure Gem Stickers

BIBLE STORY REVIEW

To review Bible story, students complete "Jesus Forgives Zacchaeus" activity on Session 4 page. **How did Jesus show God's love to Zacchaeus?** (By talking to him. By forgiving him.) **How did Zacchaeus show he was sorry for cheating people?** (Promised to give half of his money to the poor. Promised to pay back four times the money he'd taken unfairly.) **Jesus knew Zacchaeus was sorry for the wrong things he'd done. So Jesus showed God's love to Zacchaeus by forgiving him. God loves and forgives us, too!**

Indicate the Daily Treasure logo on the page. **Today's Daily Treasure reminds us that "God's Love Is Forgiving." Because God loves us, He will always forgive us when we ask Him. And because we love God, we can ask Him to help us forgive others, too.**

MEMORY VERSE/APPLICATION

Students turn Session 4 page over. Lead students in saying 1 Corinthians 13:5-6 aloud together. Then have different groups of students say the verse together. **Stand up and say the verse if you (have brown hair).** Repeat as time allows, using other descriptions (like to play games, like to read, have a brother, have a sister, etc.). (Optional: Give each student a SonTreasure Gem Sticker to place next to the memory verse.) **What does this verse mean when it talks about "keeping a record of wrongs"?** (Remembering bad things others have done. Holding a grudge.) **When we forgive someone, we don't hold a grudge. We show God's love when we forgive others for the wrong things they do to us. What is something you can do to show someone you've forgiven them?** (Say, "I forgive you." Ask them to play with you. Sit together at lunch. Give the person a compliment.)

Students complete "Trouble in Paradise" activity. **Joe must have been very upset that his sister broke his snorkel. What could happen if Joe didn't forgive Rhonnie?** (They could continue fighting. They wouldn't play together. Their parents would be upset.) **We can always tell God about our feelings and ask for His help when it's hard to forgive someone.**

PRAYER

Silently think of someone you have a hard time forgiving or showing God's love to. Let's take a moment to pray silently. You can ask God to help you forgive that person and to help you show His love to him or her. Allow a few moments for silent prayer. Close prayer time by thanking God that He forgives us when we ask and that we can show His love by forgiving others.

Jesus Lives Forever

SCRIPTURE

Mark 14:27—16:20; Luke 22:47—24:53; John 21:15-17

BIBLE MEMORY VERSE

*[Love] always protects, always trusts, always hopes, always perseveres.
Love never fails.* 1 Corinthians 13:7-8

LESSON FOCUS

God's love never fails.

BIBLE AIMS

During this session, each student may
1. DISCOVER that Jesus died and rose again so that we can experience
   God's love and be in His family forever;
2. DESCRIBE situations in which it helps to remember God's love;
3. THANK God for offering him or her God's eternal love through
   His Son, Jesus;
4. PRAY to become a member of God's family, as the Holy Spirit leads.

TEACHER'S DEVOTIONAL

How many times have we promised that our love and friendship would last forever? A childhood friend, a high school sweetheart, a college roommate. Something in us makes us want to pledge to love forever—even if we have done so before and seen that love come to an end. Perhaps this is because we were made by God to give and to receive a love that is true and lasting.

Being created in God's own image endowed us to receive God's love and to love Him in return. God's original plan for us was a love relationship that would last forever. Although this plan was broken through our sin, we still consistently desire to love forever. But we cannot know the true and lasting love God wants us to experience until we receive Jesus Christ as our Lord and our Savior. Only He can remove the sin barrier to open the way to the Father. And although our love frequently falters, God's love never fails.

Before this week is over, make sure every child in your circle of influence understands the reality of God's forever love. Each child needs to know that our desire for a relationship that lasts forever was put there by God. And when we become members of God's family, nothing will ever separate us from His love. What a reward it will be to experience the forever love of heaven with these young ones!

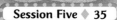

1. Set the Story (5-10 minutes)

If you only have 25 minutes for this center, omit Set the Story.

OPTION A: GEM HUNT

PREPARATION: For each team of three or four players, copy Gem Cards onto a different color of paper. Cut cards apart. Tape colored paper that matches each set of cards onto each container. Place containers far apart in different areas of classroom.

PROCEDURE: Give each student a drinking straw. Students divide into teams of three or four players. Assign each team a color and point out the container with that color taped to it.

Students form a circle. Stand in the center of the circle and toss cards into the air. When cards settle, say, "Go!" Teams race to find all cards in their team's color. When a student finds a card of his or her team's color, student sucks on drinking straw to pick up card and carry it to his or her team's container. The first team to collect all 10 cards may select a card and describe when they might use or depend on the item pictured. Invite another team to tell why they can't depend on the item forever. Gather cards and repeat game as time allows.

KEY CONVERSATION: What object is on your card? When might you depend on a (computer)? Why can't you depend on a (computer) forever? (It will become outdated. It will eventually break down.) **We depend on many things that can fail. But one thing never fails: God's love for us!**

OPTION B: BEACH BALL VOLLEYBALL

Materials Checklist
- Bible
- Session 5 Memory Verse Poster from Elementary Teaching Resources
- yarn, clothesline or game net
- masking tape
- beach ball

PREPARATION: Display Session 5 Memory Verse Poster where students can see it while playing game. Place two chairs several feet apart in the middle of the activity area. Use masking tape to secure a length of yarn, clothesline or game net between chairs.

PROCEDURE: Students divide into two teams. Teams go to either side of the net, space themselves evenly and sit down. Students play a game like volleyball, while remaining seated. Students have three hits to get ball over the net. Every time the ball goes over the net, students say a word of the verse, referring to poster as needed. If the ball hits the ground before the verse is complete, team winning that round repeats entire verse. As time and interest allow, play additional rounds with students switching sides. (Optional: If possible, play game outside on a volleyball court or in a sand area.)

KEY CONVERSATION: How might we feel when something we really like gets broken or stops working? God wants us to know that His love for us never stops. What does the word "persevere" mean? (To not give up.) **God wants us to know that even though other things may break or fail us, His love will never fail! Jesus made it possible for us to become members of God's family and experience God's love forever.**

2. Tell the Story
(10 minutes)

Materials Checklist

♦ Session 5 Bible Story Poster from Elementary Teaching Resources

♦ Post-it Notes

For each student and teacher—
♦ Bible

PREPARATION: Display Session 5 Bible Story Poster. Use Post-it Notes to mark Mark 14—16 in students' Bibles.

STORYTELLING TIP: Take time to practice telling your Bible stories aloud. Use a video or audio recorder, tell the story to a family member, or even practice storytelling in front of a mirror. The more you practice, the more relaxed and comfortable you will be. Since you won't have to struggle to recall story details, you'll be able to focus on capturing the attention of your students. And everyone will enjoy the story more!

JESUS LIVES FOREVER
Mark 14:27—16:20; Luke 22:47—24:53; John 21:15-17

Introduction
Has someone you cared about ever moved away? Did you ever have to move and leave your friends? Volunteers respond. **Today we're going to hear about a time when Jesus' friends left Him!**

Peter Declares His Loyalty
For three years, Jesus' friends traveled with Him wherever He went. They were with Jesus when He talked about God. They were with Jesus when He made sick people well. They did EVERYTHING with Jesus.

One night, Jesus told His friends that soon they would all leave Him. **How would you feel if your best friend had said something like that to you?** Jesus' friends were shocked! Jesus' friend Peter said even if everyone else left, he would ALWAYS stick by Jesus! But Jesus said that THREE times that very night—before the rooster crowed twice—Peter would deny he'd ever known Jesus. Peter didn't believe Jesus. "Even if I have to die with You," Peter said, "I will never deny You!"

Later that night, Jesus and His friends went into a garden to pray. Soldiers came with torches and swords. They grabbed Jesus and said Jesus was under arrest. Peter rushed forward, drew his sword and cut off a soldier's ear! But Jesus stopped Peter. Jesus even healed the man's ear.

Peter must have been afraid about what might happen to Jesus. But Peter was probably more afraid about what might happen to HIM. *What if they come to arrest me?* Peter must have wondered. *They might kill me!* Most of Jesus' friends were so afraid that they ran away. **Read Mark 14:53 to find out where the soldiers took Jesus.**

Peter Denies Jesus
Peter followed as the soldiers took Jesus. It was a cold night, so Peter stayed in the courtyard and warmed himself by the fire.

Suddenly, a servant girl looked at him carefully. She asked, "Aren't you one of the men who was with Jesus?" Everyone looked at Peter. Now he must have been REALLY afraid!

"I don't know what you're talking about" Peter answered. Then he got up and started to walk away.

Then someone said, "I'm sure he's one of the men who travel with Jesus!"

"It wasn't me," Peter protested, "I don't know Him."

After a little while other people said, "Sure! You must be one of Jesus' friends. You're from Galilee!"

"Look!" Peter said angrily, "I don't know the man you're talking about! Leave me alone!" Just then, Peter heard a rooster crow. Suddenly, he remembered Jesus had told him this would happen. Peter felt so sad, he cried.

Bible Storytelling Option

Give a paper plate and a fist-sized lump of play dough to each student. Students make objects as the story is being told. As you tell the story, have another teacher or helper lead students in making the following objects: numeral 3 (for Peter's three denials and Jesus' three questions), flame shapes (for the courtyard fire), cross (for Jesus' crucifixion), cave and rock (for Jesus' tomb) and cloud (for Jesus' ascension).

Even though the Roman governor knew that Jesus had done nothing wrong, he followed the wishes of Jesus' enemies and sentenced Jesus to die. Jesus knew His death was part of God's great plan to take the punishment for all our sins, and so He allowed them to kill Him on a cross. After He died, one of the soldiers realized something important. **Read Mark 15:39 to find out what the soldier learned.**

Jesus was buried in a tomb. A tomb is like a little cave cut into a hill. A large rock was rolled in front of its opening. Early Sunday morning, some women who loved Jesus went to the tomb. But when they got there, the rock had been rolled aside and Jesus was gone! They saw an angel who told them that Jesus was alive! They were afraid, but they hurried back to tell Jesus' friends what had happened. **How do you suppose Jesus' friends reacted to the women's story?**

When Peter and John heard the women's story, they couldn't believe it was true! Then their friend Mary Magdalene came to tell them that she had actually seen Jesus. What exciting news! Jesus was alive!

Later Jesus' friends were having supper together. Suddenly, Jesus was in the room with them! He WAS alive! Jesus showed them His hands and feet, where the nails had been. They touched Him! He ate with them and talked with them. Jesus told them that although He would soon be going back to heaven, and even though they wouldn't be able to see Him, He would be with them forever!

Peter Is Forgiven

Sometime later, Jesus' friends saw Jesus again while fishing in Galilee. Jesus asked Peter, "Do you love Me more than anything else?"

Peter answered, "Of course I do!"

Jesus then told Peter to care for His followers.

Then Jesus asked Peter again, "Do you love Me more than anything else?" Three times, Jesus asked Peter. And all three times, Peter said he loved Jesus. All three times, Jesus told Peter to care for the people who loved Him. Jesus wanted Peter to know that God's love is forever and that Peter needed to continue showing God's love to others.

One day, Jesus asked His friends to tell all the people in the world about His love. Then Jesus rose up and disappeared into a cloud in the sky. **Mark 16:20 tells us what Peter and Jesus' other friends did after that.**

Conclusion

Jesus promised His friends that even though they wouldn't be able to see Him, He would always love them and be with them. Jesus promises us the same thing, too! Every day there are times when we can remember God's love. Getting to know about God's love is as exciting as finding a great treasure! Jesus came to Earth and died on the cross to take the punishment for the wrong things we do. But Jesus came back to life! And because He is alive, we know He will keep His promise to love and be with all the people in God's family, now and forever! Because Jesus paid the price for all our sins, we only need to be sorry for what we have done and then ask God to give us His forgiveness so that we can become members of His family. Invite children interested in knowing more about becoming members of God's family to talk with you or another teacher after class. (See "Leading a Child to Christ," p. 8.)

3. Apply the Story (10-15 minutes)

Materials Checklist

♦ colored markers

For each student—

♦ Session 5 Treasure Guide page

Optional—
♦ SonTreasure Gem Stickers

BIBLE STORY REVIEW

Why did Peter cry? (He had denied Jesus was his friend. He said He didn't know Jesus.) **What did Jesus ask Peter to do?** (Take care of the people who love Jesus.)

To review Bible story, students complete "Jesus Lives Forever" activity on Session 5 page. **What does the first Bible-story picture show?** (Jesus praying in the garden.) **What does the second Bible-story picture show?** (Jesus being arrested.) Continue for each Bible-story picture. **Jesus died on the cross so that we can be forgiven for the wrong things that we do. Jesus died because He loves us. But Jesus didn't stay dead, He came back to life! Jesus lives and loves us forever!**

Indicate the Daily Treasure logo on the page. **Our Daily Treasure reminds us that "God's Love Is Forever." This means that God loves us now, and He will keep loving us forever. His love for us will never end!**

MEMORY VERSE/APPLICATION

Students turn Session 5 page over. Lead students in saying the verse: All boys say the first word, all girls say the second, boys say the third, and so on. As time allows, repeat verse several times, alternating which group says the first word. (Optional: Give each student a SonTreasure Gem Sticker to place next to the memory verse.) **What does the word "persevere" mean?** (It means to continue to do something even when it's hard. To keep trying.) **This verse tells us that God's love continues all the time. God's love never fails! We can become members of God's family and experience His love forever.**

Briefly tell a time when remembering God's love has been helpful to you. Then lead students to complete "Remember When . . ." activity. **Everyone experiences times when it really helps to remember God's love. There are times when we're lonely, afraid, worried or just don't know what to do. There are times when we're glad to know that God loves us and is always with us.**

PRAYER

The greatest gift of love ever given was when God gave us His Son, Jesus, to die for our sins. When we believe in Jesus and admit our sins to God, He promises to forgive us and make us part of His family. Lead students in silently thanking God for His love and for offering us the gift of salvation through Jesus.

If you were on an island, would you rather eat a coconut or an octopus?

If you were on an island, would you rather see a dolphin or a whale?

If you were on an island, would you rather ride in a sailboat or ride the waves on a boogie board?

If you were on an island, would you rather climb a palm tree or go for a hike in a tropical rain forest?

If you were on an island beach, would you rather search for seashells or buried treasure?

If you were on an island, would you rather build a sand castle or nap on a beach towel?

If you were on an island, would you rather swim in the ocean or slide down a waterfall?

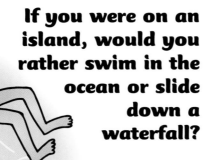

If you were on an island, would you rather hear a parrot squawk or see a crab walk?

"This is how God showed his love

among us: He sent his one

and only Son into the world

that we might live through him."

1 John 4:9

"Love is patient,

love is kind.

It does not envy,

it does not boast,

it is not proud."

1 Corinthians 13:4

 **" [Love]**

 **is**

not

 **rude,**

it

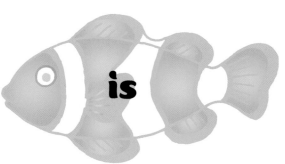 **is**

 **not**

 **self-seeking."**

1 Corinthians

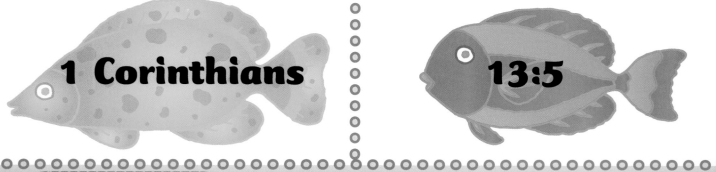 **13:5**

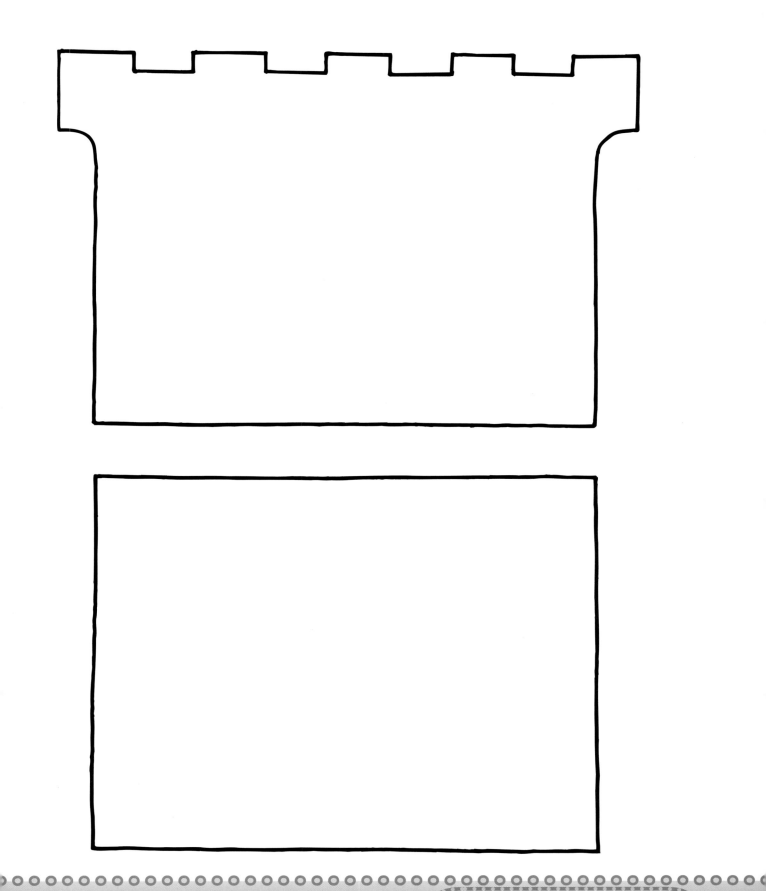

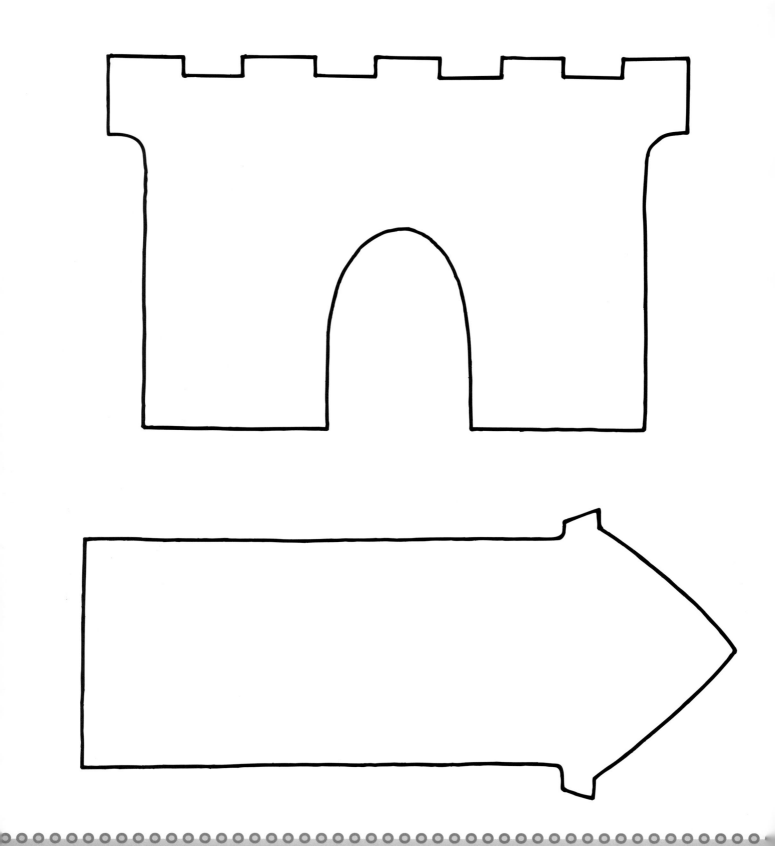

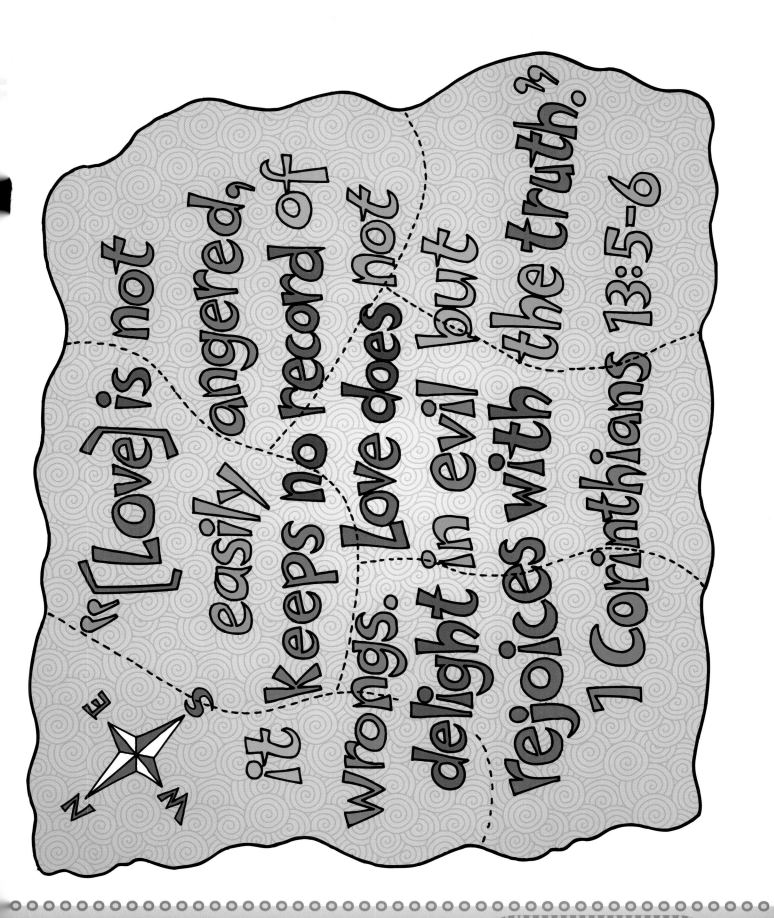

"…[Love] is not easily angered, it keeps no record of wrongs. Love does not delight in evil but rejoices with the truth." 1 Corinthians 13:5-6

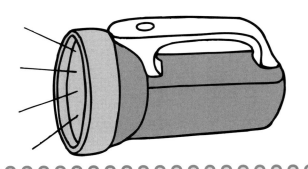
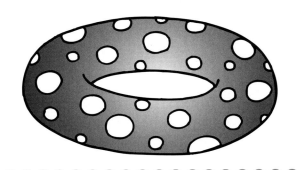

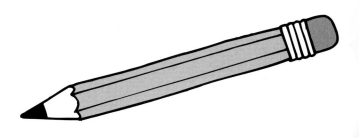

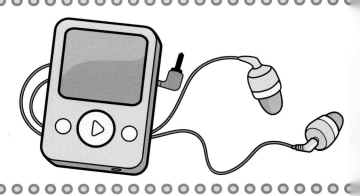

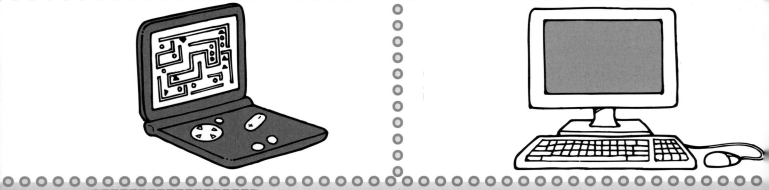